The
Sound of
Paint Drying

Also by John Hegley

Glad to Wear Glasses
Can I Come Now, Dad?
Five Sugars Please
These Were Your Father's
Love Cuts
The Family Pack
Beyond Our Kennel
Dog

www.johnhegley.co.uk

The
Sound of
Paint Drying

John Hegley

Methuen

This edition first published in the United Kingdom in 2009
by Methuen

10 9 8 7 6 5 4 3 2

Copyright © 2003, 2009 by John Hegley

ISBN 978 0 413 73180 7

John Hegley has asserted his right under
the Copyright, Designs and Patents Act, 1988,
to be identified as the author of this work.

Methuen
8 Artillery Row
SW1P 1RZ

www.methuen.co.uk

Methuen Publishing Limited Reg. No. 3543167

A CIP catalogue record for this book is available
from the British Library

Designed by Bryony Newhouse

Printed and bound in Great Britain by
TJ International Ltd, Padstow, Cornwall

Thanks to BBC Radio 4 where some of the enclosed pieces first surfaced, and to Keith Moore who shaded the drawing on page 32.

Contents

IT'S DOG EAT DOG
OUT THERE

May 2002

In the doctor's reception the sign read:
Are you looking after someone over 65
with mental health problems?
I read the sign as:
Are you looking for someone over 65
with mental health problems?

The knowledge

I have known a love
which was true.
I have been beautiful
in the eyes of the beautiful.
I have been kissed by the lips I longed for.
I have seen heaven
in the eyes of the beholder.
I have been home.

Quick potato poem

The spud
sped.

Hats off to Luton

An imagined dialogue between my mum and dad the day they moved to Luton in the mid-1950s. They had been living in London up until then, where I believe they had been very happy together.

Roman letters are Dad talking, italics are Mum's words.

They used to fashion hats here, years ago,
they did, you know,
they fashioned hats of very high renown.

However many hats here, do you know?
Every day a sea of hats,
sufficient hats to drown.

So has it dried up totally?
Not totally, but certainly, the modern-day production
is significantly down.

So now, how many hats, here?
I don't know . . .
a puddle not an ocean
but they're still of high renown.

The town has lost a livelihood . . .
the team are still the Hatters though . . .
it matters not how good they are at football as a game.
And also there's a boating hat
that people call a Luton Hat . . .
unless of course they're people
who don't know the boater's name.

The fashion has been rationed now
there are so many people going out without a hat
and just some hair upon their crown.
But still we have our passion
and let's hope it stays in fashion
if it don't, I'll buy a Luton Hat and eat my hat
and after that,
I'll get sat on the privy
and I'll flush the boater down.

Left-footed poem

My left foot at football
was my least good.
Being as my right foot was bad,
this meant that my left foot
was very bad.
There were occasions, though,
when a combination
of self-belief and bravado
had me use my very bad foot
with thunderous accuracy.
On one occasion in Kilkenny
during a match between comedians,
Ireland against the rest of the world,
we, the non-Irish,
were an embarrassing 7-2 down
when the ball came whizzing my way
and I had an impulse to play
the left-footed dilettante
and the ball flew emphatically, unstoppably
beyond the reach of the flailing goalkeeper.
My own goalkeeper.
And I took ownership of that goal
instead of feeling small;
I celebrated what I'd done.
We were, after all,
comedians.

The Luton bungalow circa 1963

Today I got some bamboo from the ironmonger. I made a longbow out of the long bit and used the short bits for firing. I shot one at my sister and it hit her just above the eye. I didn't mean to. I was aiming for her neck.

*

Today I went to get my eyes tested. I have not been able to see the filthy magazines on the top shelf of the Co-op properly.

*

Today I got a letter from Jacques, my pen friend at the petrol station in France. I have written him three long letters and he has not replied. Today he asked me not to write to him any more.

*

Today, Sir hit Richard Jones
with his bamboo cane
and it split.
At playtime I said, 'Richard Jones
has got hard bones.'
Everybody laughed.
And then I added, 'But not as hard as stones.'
Nobody laughed at the new bit.
I had overdone it.

*

Today I wore my new glasses. Tortoiseshell ones. My
brother said a tortoise wouldn't be seen dead in my
new glasses.

*

At school today, Jane had her thick black tights on.
I love her in these; they are called Hugmebunnies, but
I don't tell her I love her in these. And I don't tell her
I love her.

Yesterday I became a shelver in the Luton Central
Library. It is heavingly monotonous work, but I dream
of Jane coming in one day and seeing me in my job

and my badge and my library, and in this new world I
am able to express my love and we chat and laugh and
kiss and the shelves can go and stuff themselves.

*

Last night it was Bonfire Night
and we pretended our guy
was Mr McMaster.
Today my sister told the priest
what we had done,
and later on he said to me,
'John, I understand you burned an effigy
of Mr McMaster.'
I was ashamed.
'Yes, Father,' I said, 'we did,'
and he said, 'Good.'

*

Yesterday our new dog arrived
He is a beagle,
a hunting dog.
Last night we had the discussion about his name.
My brother said he was going out on his motorbike;

he said he didn't care what the dog was called.
I told him it is very important
a dog's name.
The name you give your dog
is the name it will keep for all of its life,
unless you decide to change it,
but how often do people change the name of their dog?
No matter how naughty it is
a dog's name is for always,
and if it runs away without a tag
and new people take it in,
if you thought about the name properly
the new people will think of the same name as you,
    because it is the essence of the dog.
And I looked into the coals of fire
and the coals of the dog's eyes
and a name came
a word I did not even know,
somehow it came.
The name I chose
was Temnos.
We have called him Hunter.

*

Today before I went to Cubs
I went scrumping apples

But they were cookers not eaters.
Even though they were sour
I ate fourteen of them.
On the bus home I had an accident in my trousers.

*

Today, it was Christmas. At night, Dad was smoking a cigar and me and Angela were looking at our presents and my brother was having a glass of beer with my dad. He is eighteen now, so he can have beer. I had a try but didn't like it. How can they like it? Mum was eating toffee. It was great, all of us being together and nobody getting annoyed. I took Hunter up the road for a walk. There were stars. I was glad to be me. It was a big feeling. Bigger than the sky. The big dark sky.

*

When I was little my brother used to take me out
    with him.
Now, he has a life without me, but I understand.
He is eighteen. I am ten.
At least we still have the same bedroom
and on Saturday we read my comics together.

And he lets me ride on the back of his motorbike,
and I hold on to him very tightly.

Today my foot got caught in my brother's motorbike
wheel. It's only a Honda 50 but it hurt. I had to go to
the Luton and Dunstable Hospital to have it stitched
up. The bone was showing in my heel. I kept saying,
'It's terribly bad, it's terribly bad!' The nurse hit me
and told me to shut up.

*

Today I flicked
my cocoa at the wall
with the teaspoon
as I lay in my bed.
I wasn't sure where it landed
but, later, my mum dragged me back
to witness the lashed splashings on the wallpaper,
telling me to just wait until my father came in.

My dad did not see it as an artistic improvement,
a departure from the norm,
an embellishment of the found,
a playing with the form,
and he printed the shape
of his writing hand

on my short-trousered skin,
when he came in.

*

On Saturday me and my dad went to confession
    together.
I asked him what he'd confessed;
he said he told the priest
he'd lost his temper with me, again.

Today we went to London
on the train for a day out.
Just me and my dad.
I wondered why it wasn't all of us.
I think maybe the priest
has told him to spend a day with his son on his own
as a penance.

*

Today at the church bazaar Mr McMaster was running
the drop-a-penny-in-the-bucket-of-water-and-cover-
another-coin-to-win-it stall.
    When my penny plopped, I looked down and saw

that it had landed right on the big prize of half a crown. When I went to take out my winnings, Mr McMaster said, 'You can't have it – it's not completely covered.' I said, 'How can it be completely covered, a penny is smaller than half a crown.' Taking my penny out of the water and handing it back to me, Mr McMaster said, 'I tell you what – if you want to argue with adults, you can go and spend your money some-where else.'

Today I asked my mum
if she would shelter me
if I killed someone.
She said that she would
but she wouldn't be
    very pleased about it.

Poem about unrequited trying
to get off with someone

Treading earth
in the Belfast Botanic Gardens
he looked as the greenery grew,
with a growing sense of his slowliness
on the previous evening with you.
He didn't get far
in the public bar
in spite of the light that grew,
and lying alone in his berth, that night,
all of his troubles were you.
You'd had your violin
underneath your chin
in that little theatre in Queens';
he said he'd got into your playing
and he wanted to get into your jeans.

And your hair.

And your heartbeat.

He was a man apart in the Botanic Gardens,
unseeing the scenery grow.
He'd been given a chance
in Belfast.
And he was well slow.

Ruled by the wrong emotion

I was a London boy
living in Luton Town,
I was ten years old
and I would frown the whole day through.
I had the hots for you,
to use an inadequate phrase,
but I kept it undisclosed.
Was it just that girls weren't cool?
Or was it a fear of rejection?
Was it self-protection?
Or was it my predilection
for being a fool,
around the school?

Jane, Jane, Jane
I called you every name
except the one I wanted to,
I never called you Jane.
I was the second best fighter in the class,
who'd be number one?
Reckoned to be the second best fighter
but I had the thirty-second most fun.
Kicking you instead of kissing you
missing out on your smile
always being vile,

instead of singing a song for you
the way I wanted to.

Jane, Jane, Jane
I wouldn't explain
the way I loved the way you were,
the way you surprised me
when you took that bamboo cane
without a whimper.
Kicking instead of kissing,
missing out by a mile
bringing up the bile
instead of singing a song for you
the way I wanted to,
the way I wanted you
all the while.

Jane, Jane, Jane
you put the wind in my sails
and I blew it out again.
Jane, Jane, Jane
I'll see you again
and I will explain,
I'll say your name:
I won't call you Smellypants
I won't call you Smellypoo
unless you want me to.

Concrete man

I'm all hard hat me,
not Mr Softy,
no … Mr Safety – Mr Health and Safety.
I'm a roving rep,
I watch your step,
I make construction criticism.
I case the joints,
I get the gist
of joist and girder.
I crane my neck,
I check and check
and treble check.
I save some lives.
I troubleshoot
the rubble-shoot.
I head for heights,
I'm a roving rep,
it's a bit of a schlep
but I take it in my stride.
Mile after mile
after what's been botched
and what's been missed
but the closed fist
of financial resistance
and the stench

of I couldn't give a monkey wrench,
makes the Roving Rep a
leper.
In their mill
they can do without my kind of grist:
the only prob
with the job at the moment is
it don't exist.

Beer man

I saw a beer man,
saw him appear, man,
the kind of man
whose hair
is unaware
of the existence
of the brush, a man
who wouldn't rush
to buy a comb.
The kind of man
you'd find would be resistant
towards any kind of cleaning
round the home,
if he had one.

So, what was he doing on a mobile phone?

He was a beer man,
he had a beer can
held against his ear, man.

By rail, Scotland

I am sat on the train opposite an attractive woman of maybe eighty. We have been chatting cheerfully. She is Mrs Phelps, Mrs Dora Phelps; she is on her way back from a Christian singles weekend. One phrase in her description of the event sticks with me: 'Fun and Fellowship'. She remains glued to the passing land-scape, unwraps a sweet and is soon sucking fervently. I feel the conversation has been going well enough for me to ask her: 'Can I have one?' She looks at me directly, for the first time now – 'No. Get your own sweets.'

'Fun and Fellowship ... like the Cathars,' I suggest.

'The Cathars?' says Mrs Phelps, pushing me back into the headrest, because I am obscuring her view of the landscape.

I nod and continue. 'The Cathars were Christian heretics in the Middle Ages. A million wiped out by Simon de Montfort, a million!'

'How strange,' she says, '... so exact a number.'

She speaks of the second coming and says she wishes the Lord would 'rattle his dags' and get down here. I ask her what dags are and she says that it is best not to ask.

She gives me details of the next gathering, writing the address on a sweet wrapper. I wonder what sort of pen she is using that writes so readily on waxed paper. She hands me a photograph of herself wearing merely a pair of pants. 'That's me half a century ago, when I was twenty-six.'

I feel an impossible desire, which is at the same time infinitely comforting. I think of the song recently released by the Beautiful South, which boasts the un-witherable beauty of the eyes.

As we pull into her station, we exchange phone numbers, although I give her the wrong one because it's all a bit too frightening.

The totel hotel experience, Scotland

Not all the dress was fancy
at the fancy-dress event
some just went the way they were
and others never went.
Someone took a felt-tip pen
and blackened out a lens
and she became a pirate
in the mirror
in the Men's.
There was a family who dressed up
like some cowboys on a ranch,
and someone was a tree
by simply carrying a branch.
And someone dressed as God's own son
and walked across the lake,
but he wore a pair of glasses
so you saw that he was fake.
The Maître d' himself it was
who dressed up in this way
and someone said, 'It's sacrilege,'
the Maître d' said, 'Nay,
irreverence – there's a difference.'
And to the two who came as Monk and Nun
the Maître d' said, 'Gad,
I hope you've got good habits,'

but their habits they were bad:
just a couple of blankets,
with safety-pinned pillow cases
masquerading as hoods.

The next morning at the hotel, John looked at Tony's itinerary, to find there was nothing scheduled before the evening appearance of Dynamite (musical duo). He asked of the passing Maître d' ...

'Are there any activities scheduled for today?'

'Yes, there's the musical duo, "Dynamite".'

This was not enough for John – 'But that's tonight. What about today?'

The Maître d' expanded. 'There's reading in the lounge. Reading material is provided in both the form of newspapers, and I'm talking about today's newspapers, as current as you can get, and also of course, for reading of a more archival nature, there are the books upon the shelving. Guests have completely open access thereunto.'

And with that the Maître d' was gone, moved on.

'Tony, could you pass the toast.'

'So, John, you're having the piece of toast, are you?'

'Mm ... do you think one piece of toast between two is a little meagre?'

Tony responded smartly to his friend's complaint.

'We were down late, John. I think they've been very accommodating. Breakfast is supposed to finish at eight o'clock. We come waltzing in at a minute past and still they serve us.'

'What do you mean, waltz? There was no dancing upon our entrance.'

'Dancing is more than just a movement of feet, John. It is an inner movement of the people which may or may not be translated into physical motion; on this occasion it was not.' With that, Tony divided the slice of toast in two, giving one piece to himself and the other to his top pocket for consumption at a later moment. 'I'm going out to feed the birds, John.'

After breakfast, John remained lounging in the lounge, beginning his reading activities with a look at the morning newspaper, while Tony went out to feed the birds.

Tony wasn't back for lunch, so John ate alone; taking a Polaroid photograph of both his main course and his dessert, so that Tony could see what he had missed. He didn't bother trying to capture the tomato soup or the coffee, as these he felt could be adequately described wordly. At the next table there was the couple who'd won the fancy-dress competition with their portrayal of Neptune and a mermaid. They had both worn professional wigs, which in Mrs Mermaid's case was four feet in length. Towards the evening's end, John had heard the cowboy making a lewd remark to the barman about her not wearing a top. John wanted to counteract this immaturity, as he saw it, and had loudly told her that he found her costume cheerfully risqué, only for the overhearing Neptune to hoist off John's spectacles with his trident.

'Do you fancy a threesome later on?' said the mermaid when her husband had gone to pay a visit. 'Our marriage is on the rocks,' explained the watery one.

'I'm all right, thanks. Thanks all the same.' said John. Neptune returned and said to John, 'Do you fancy a threesome later on?' John politely declined and once more had his spectacles removed by the volatile sea god.

That was on the previous evening, now the pair were quietly involved in their meals, with little time for anyone or anything else. John proceeded with his own luncheon and his photography, without awkwardness or discontent.

After lunch, John decided to deviate from the reading option and give attention to cleaning his spectacles. He tucked himself into a seat beside the open fire. Beneath the neighbouring armchair, Hamish the dog sat beside its owner, the human. John lumped a log on to the burning; the sparks flew. John was enthusiastic.

'It's lovely, an open fire, isn't it?'

'Mm,' answered the owner.

'I liked your farmer's outfit at the fancy dress last night.'

'It wasn't an outfit, I just put some lipstick on my cheeks and tucked my socks into my trousers.'

'*And* tied a hanky around your neck.'

'Yes.'

'Very swanky. Whose lipstick was it?'

'I borrowed it from the pirate lady in our toilet.'

'That was very generous for a pirate,' said John, leaving the dog owner feeling he had nowhere to go in the conversation. John looked at the dog.

'If he'd been a Border collie you'd have looked even more like a farmer.'

Although Hamish's owner had opted out of the exchange, John leant forward in his chair and began talking intently and at length. He cleaned his spectacles as he spoke. Hamish cleaned his privates.

'My father used to warn me about talking to strangers, I remember once we were sat over an outdoor café table, close to a canal. "And just because it's short, doesn't mean it shouldn't be sharp, John," he said. He'd just been speaking about how you were less likely to lose a small stub of pencil than a long brand new one. I said, "That's probably true, Dad, but it doesn't make much sense, does it?"

'"There's a lot that doesn't make much sense, John," my dad said.'

John paused in his tale and looked into the eyes of the former farmer for response. The man got up without a word, and moved in the direction of the toilets, followed by the barking.

'How was it, Tone?' said John referring to his returning companion's excursion. 'I thought you were only going to feed the birds, but it's nearly four now!'

'I went to the pub and had a game of dominoes with some of the local people.'

'Oh, I wish you'd come and got me. I'd love to have joined in.'

'Sometimes a man needs to be alone, John.'

'But you weren't alone, were you? You were engaging local people in domineering activities.'

'Look, I'll give you a game, later. Please, don't feel

you need to be implicated in every aspect of my life. It draws me away from you.'

'Here, Tone, I took some photos of the meal you missed.'

'That was thoughtful of you. Let's have a look.'

John let him see and Tony said it was a very novel idea, but was disappointed not to see a photo of the soup, as he found John's description of it to be inadequate as well as inedible.

That evening John was to get a surprise. He had thought that the last time he'd seen Mrs Phelps would indeed be the last, but here she was in the hotel lounge, drawing on to a potato.

'Let's talk about betrayal,' said Mrs Phelps, using her thumbnail to chip off a limpet of mud from the spud. The wrong phone number he'd purposely given her at their last meeting had come home to be counted. 'Do you know whose number it was?' she said. 'It was a woman whose dog had recently passed away. When I asked if I could speak to John, she started crying because John was the name of her recently deceased dog.'

'I'm sorry. I'm sorry,' John told her, 'but how could I have known?'

'You didn't need to know, because you didn't need to give me the wrong number, did you?'

'Forgive me.'

'Forgetting you would be preferable. It was pathetic.'

At that moment Tony tumbled cheerily into the room.

'Hi, folks, I hope I'm not disturbing you.'

'It's me that's disturbing,' adjudged Mrs Phelps.

'I'll pop back a little later on,' decided Tony, making a speedy exit, ignoring the pitched potato which struck him in the back of beyond.

'You gave me the wrong number, John,' Mrs Phelps continued.

'We've established that,' John defended.

'Don't try your rationalising strategies.'

'OK. I thought if I gave you the wrong number you could at least think that I did it by mistake and not see it as a rejection.'

'But people know their own phone number, don't they, so how would I think it was a mistake?'

'I said I'd recently moved before I gave it to you – so that you could think it was just a tragic mistake; I'd recently moved and misremembered,' petitioned John.

'I'm going up, it's late,' said Mrs Phelps.

'It's eight o'clock,' protested John.

'Five past,' corrected Mrs Phelps.

Mrs Phelps moved towards the door, which John held open, watching her elderly frame safely up the stairs before turning towards the music room.

In the music room, the duo had everybody up and dancing. Unfortunately that was another duo on another evening. Tonight Tony was dancing alone. John entered and motioned Tony to stop dancing and sit down, now that the duo had stopped playing. Producing an oblong box, Tony suggested dominoes, and the heart-warming rattle that betokened a game's beginning quickly followed that box's opening.

They were midway through their second game, Tony had just knocked on the table, when the Maître d' suddenly burst upon the attention, crying, 'Mrs Phelps has been assassinated! Nobody leave the room. This is a case for Sherlock Holmes.'

'*Who* is Mrs Phelps?' demanded the ex-cowboy.

'Who *was* Mrs Phelps,' corrected the Maître d'. 'She was a late arrival, an older lady,' he continued.

'How did she die?' continued the cowboy.

'What I assume to be the weapon was found beside

her body, it was a crossbow customised to accommodate the firing of potatoes with drawings on them.'

'Listen here,' said the cowboy, 'I'm not satisfied with this mystery at all, in fact the whole place is a let-down. I'm disappointed with this duo, they're not dynamite at all, and I've already moved rooms twice on account of blood on the net curtains and Mr Lewis's incessant barking.'

'It's my dog barking, not me, it's Hamish,' whimpered Mr Lewis. The carping cowboy continued his accusations in the direction of the Maître d'.

'Look, just tell me why we've got a murder mystery with a guest that nobody knows, with a stupid weapon.'

'It's only a bit of fun,' said the former fancy-dress pirate.

'A very small bit of fun,' replied the one-time cowboy.

'Why don't we wait and see what happens when Sherlock Holmes gets here?' the pirate continued.

'Is Doctor Watson coming too?' asked Hamish's owner, hopefully.

'They probably haven't budgeted for him,' sneered the cowboy.

'Why don't you stop complaining and let the other guests recover from the shock of terrible news,' arbitrated the Maître d'. 'I think perhaps it might help calm the nerves if our duo were to strike up their tunes once more.'

There was a mumble of dissent, as the duo struck up their tunes once more. The duo called 'Dynamite'.

Tony and John invited the Maître d' to join them at doms, but he declined on the grounds that it was disrespectful to the band, and also to the dead. He then departed to keep watch for the arrival of the famous detective.

John and Tony took the hint, put away their dotted oblongs and attempted to see virtue in the songs of the duo. There was no encore; in fact, sensitive to the desultory mood of the audience, they volunteered to do one less: this met with a genuine round of appreciation. The dominant member of the pair then announced the arrival of Sherlock Holmes, at which a familiar deerstalkered figure entered into the company.

'It's the Maître d'tective,' said the cowboy, accusingly.

'Elementary, my dear tosspot' adjudged the Maître d', sliding into sleuth mode. 'Yes, I am the Sleuth, I ruthlessly seek out the truth,' he sang. Then, turning to John, he said, 'You, sir, are the number-one suspect, having once killed a flame of friendship inside this woman with your uncaring disregard.'

John overcame his horror and gave his domino alibi, which was corroborated by his companion who exhibited to the detective the felt-tipped scorekeeping of the disrupted game.

Other questions were asked of other guests; more along the lines of a general knowledge quiz than an investigation. This quizzing was brought to a conclusion when Holmes brought out a walkie-talkie.

'Hello … yes … yes … no … well, thanks for that.

'That was Watson, everyone. You'll be glad to know that resuscitation has been effected by the offices of the good doctor. He has covered the victim's body in wholemeal loaves and she has risen from the bread.' At which the duo broke into applause to signal the end of the evening's entertainment.

The next morning John and Tony were getting dressed.

'John, would you … ?' Tony asked, proffering his arm, shirted but unfastened.

'Why don't you have buttons instead of cufflinks, Tony?'

'I wouldn't need to ask for your help if I had buttons, would I?'

As he was giving linking assistance, John noticed the image of a kennel on the cufflink's surface.

Tony noticed John's noticing and showed him the other one with a dog on it.

'They're quite fun, aren't they?' said John, 'but I think I'd prefer each link to be the same.'

'The illusion of order, John – things can only be similar, not the same. Actually, I'd prefer it that way myself, but these were a gift, and that outweighs any question of taste.'

Tony put on his tie and John pulled on his fisherman neck trousers.

'So, who gave you the cufflinks, then?'

'You did, John.'

When they arrived downstairs for what was named in the itinerary as the 'pre-breakfast board meeting', Tony suggested Monopoly.

John was intrigued. 'What do you like about Monopoly?'

Tony wasn't sure. 'Well, I like the funny little tokens.'

'What, the things for going round the board you mean, are they called tokens?'

'I thought so, I'm not sure now. I don't know another name for them, so let's call them tokens, shall we?'

They took the Monopoly set and sat beside the bay window in the lounge. Very soon the rattling sound of dice-tossing and token-tapping could be heard from John and Tony's table.

On seeing Mrs Phelps come by at breakfast, John introduced her bony frame to Tony.

'Ah, Tony, sorry about the potato incident,' she said, 'it was the hooligan element coming out in me.'

'It's in all of us,' said Tony, putting her glasses into John's porridge.

'Please sit down,' said John.

'Thanky,' answered Phelpsie, cleaning them with her hanky.

'So what was all that stuff about the murder and the Maître d'?' John enquired as she cleaned.

'Oh, I've been here a few times before, and on the last occasion he asked me if I'd be the subject of his little yuletide detecting diversion, as he calls it.'

'Do I detect a certain intimacy between you two?' said John, almost accusingly.

'None,' she answered.

'He gets jealous,' said Tony.

'But not of me, surely.'

'With respect, it's never anything much to do with the other person.'

'What are you saying?' said John.

'You know what I'm saying, John. It's all to do with you and your desire to possess, and all that.'

'All what?'

'Anyway,' said Mrs Phelps divertingly, 'I agreed to do it, as long as I didn't have to go on show, and as long as he agreed to involve a potato in the incident.'

'You got your way, then?'

'I think he probably wished he hadn't asked me, though. He told me about the dissatisfaction of the guests.'

'Sleep with him, did you? Satisfy him, did you ...?' said John, suddenly turning nasty. Fortunately Mrs Phelps realised from Tony's earlier clue that she shouldn't let herself get upset by these accusations and she just gave John a quick karate chop in the front-neck to encourage him to discontinue this line of questioning. After which, the three of them sat at the table and looked out at the high, high hills.

'It *is* beautiful, isn't it,' she said.

'Yes it is,' said John rubbing his injured throat.

John's injury prevented him from joining in with the after-breakfast Haggis Hurling, throughout which Hamish barked continually. John found it amusing to note how what started out as a take-or-leave-it bit of fun, turned into a test of muscularity for the more able-bodied of the males. Handing Tony the prize of a bottle of whisky (miniature), the Maître d' added, 'And I do hope you'll have another winner for us at

Hotel with hat on hill.

tonight's gala finale. Anything up to five minutes in length, and no lewdity, as the children are being allowed to stay up for this special event.'

The Maître d' made his reindeer-horned way indoors.

'Hamish's owner has joined my church,' announced Mrs Phelps to John and Tony, on their way within.

'What church is that?' asked Tony.

'The Church of the Holy Potato. It's got two members now. Three if you count the dog,' boasted Mrs Phelps.

'I'm amazed that you got through to him,' said John. 'I couldn't. He's not a listener, is he?'

'You've got to know how to draw people in, John,' Mrs Phelps explained. 'I told him about the dogs in the Bible.'

'There aren't any, are there?' asked Tony.

'There *are* one or two, actually,' clarified John.

'There are a lot more in my version. And plenty of potatoes too,' clarified Mrs Phelps.

Later in the lounge John, Tony and Mrs Phelps were discussing a joint contribution to the gala finala. John offered his drama about the disadvantages of technology and the benefits of writing by hand, but Mrs Phelps said she couldn't read it and suggested an old routine she'd seen on her first Girl Guide campfire. This involved washing the floor with rags and buckets of water: three times the participants went off to refill the buckets, returning to do their scrubbery with contents renewed. On the third occasion, one of them looked at the floor and said, 'We can't get it any better than that. Our work here is done.' And they threw the contents of the buckets over the audience, who cowered in the expectation of water. But it was confetti.

'It would be good if we could make it different in some way,' advised Tony.

Mrs Phelps had an idea. A bright one. At which the trio's contribution was, as they say, 'sorted'.

The evening's variety show was begun by the cowboy doing a comedy routine using the checked shirt he'd used as fancy dress.

'You may wonder why I'm wearing this checked shirt. Well, it's because I've got a part-time job as a table in an Italian restaurant …'

John interrupted by saying, 'You won't be much good for dominoes then, will you?'

'Why's that then? What do you mean!?' answered the bemused performer.

John explained. 'It wouldn't be wood on wood, would it, it would be wood on a person's back covered in a shirt.'

John expected some kind of cocksure reply, but the man merely faltered.

'No … you're right … I've lost my place now … hold on …'

The Maître d' who was hosting the proceedings came on and said the cowboy could complete his story after the interval. Next on were the couple who had been Neptune and the mermaid. They did a very short song which the mermaid began.

> 'My husband and I
> don't get along at all
> the things we've got in common
> are so few ...'

And her partner finished.

> 'It's a shame there's just the two of us
> you couldn't make a queue of us,
> don't get married's my advice to you.'

'Good job we haven't got the confetti,' muttered Mrs Phelps.

'I'm sorry about earlier, mate,' said John to the cowboy at the sandwich table during the interval. 'I thought you'd give me a good old heckler's put-down. Tell me what was going to happen next in your story? I wanted to hear it.'

The cowboy obliged. John thought the audience hadn't missed anything, but out of humanity he said, 'That would have been really good, that would. I'm sorry I interrupted.'

The cowboy answered, 'Thanks – but by telling you now, I realise the story was useless, so you did me a favour by getting me to stop.'

'No problem,' said John.

'If we could reconvene,' announced the Maître d'.

'We now move on to our animal slot,' he announced. 'Before we are introduced to the creature I would just like to ask the owner a few questions.'

Hamish's owner stood up and positioned himself and his dog next to the Maître d' who asked the following list of rhetorical questions:

How long have you had your dog?

How long *is* your dog?

When you leave your dog's dirt behind, do you
    ever clean up the dirt of another dog on a
    one-to-one basis?

Would you describe your dog as lucky?

Have you ever placed a pair of spectacles on your dog;
    if so where?

What is it that makes your dog bark?

What is it that makes your dog tick?

Is your dog a stick fancier?

Does your dog make unpleasant smells?

Do you clean them up?

Do you mark them out of ten?

Is your dog actually a potato?

The tricks which followed were rather unimpressive. Hamish was told to sit, stand, sniff and bark which he continued to do beyond his owner's termination of the performance. After encouraging a generous applause, the Maître d' went swiftly on to the next routine. 'And now our very own receptionist Trevor will perform a poem of his own composing.' Which he did:

> 'I like a man
> with muscle
> and I like a bushy tash
> I like it to be tender
> and I like my own gender
> a chap's got as much right to love another chap
> as he's got to wear a back-to-front baseball cap.'

The Maître d' stood up and voiced his objection to his employee's contribution. 'That was very short, Trevor, and moving rapidly forward ...'

Upstairs in their room that evening, John and Tony chatted about the evening's cabaret diversions.

'What did you think of the turns, then, Tone? I think ours went down well.'

'Mm ... Mind you, the parents of those kids were a bit over the top about the spuds we threw over them.'

'We did give one of them mild concussion, though.'

'A potato can't have concussion, John.'

'It can in this place. Did you like what I said to them?'

'The spuds or the parents?'

'The parents: that there was no need to go over the top because the spuds were over the top of everyone, as in being above their heads, so there was no harm done.'

'I think it was above their heads, John.'

The next day was the end of it all. There would be breakfast, then time added on for packing, the Maître d's final address and home. John and Tony came away from the table and went back to their room to enclose their belongings.

With the encasing completed, they sat looking out in the lounge.

'Do you fancy a turn around the garden, Tony?'

And Tony was up without answering, in affirmation of his friend's suggestion.

Outside, as the cold made dragon-breath of their exhalations, John noticed something in the corner of the lawn.

Something wooden, half hidden, behind a large rhododendron.

'I'm surprised I never noticed this when we were doing the Haggis Hurling, Tony.'

They were looking at a very large kennel.

'Have you seen any dog in the hotel, though?' enquired John.

'Hamish?' suggested Tony.

'Apart from Hamish.'

'Hamish?' suggested Tony.

'I said *apart* from Hamish.'

'No.'

'So why is there a kennel?'

'A dog dead?'

'But why a kept kennel? It's a bit morbid, isn't it?'

'Unless they're going to get a new dog.'

'Hamish?'

'What are you talking around?'

'Maybe they want to buy Hamish.'

'He's his owner's *raison d'être*, Tony.'

'What's that?'

'A reason for living.'

'No, I meant what was that sound?'

'I didn't hear anything.'

'It sounds like monks singing.'

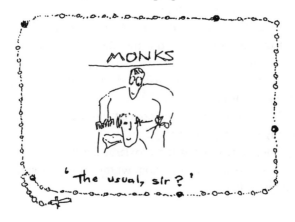

Stood before the hotel reception desk, John plied Trevor for huge kennel info. Trevor was obliging. 'It would seem that the hotel stands on the site of an ancient monastery which had a kennel attached – or was it a brothel – no, a kennel, surely. Anyway, the monastery was levelled centuries ago but the kennel was left untouched in the grounds …'

'… The House of Dog,' said the Maître d' coming out from the office, 'at least that's what the monks called it.'

'Surely they wouldn't have? That would have been blasphemy.'

'They were an unusual order. It's said the kennel in our grounds is that same kennel unscathed. Anyway, must get on – final address to prepare,' said the Maître d' getting all clipped in his talking.

John and Tony returned to the garden for a closer examination of the dog dwelling.

They arrived to find Mrs Phelps taking the air and trying to look into the huge kennel's interior.

'Any idea what it's like in there?' she asked them both.

'Why not have a look for yourself, Phelpsie,' answered John.

'Are you trying to get rid of me again?'

'I thought we'd dealt with that.'

'We're *dealing* with that,' she corrected. 'Anyway, I don't know if I can go crawling in there with my back.'

'I'd give you mine, if I could,' said Tony, only being friendly.

At this moment he saw a wheelbarrow in the opposite corner of the garden. He brought it over, tipped it downwards, then held it firm as Mrs Phelps backed into the barrow's burrow.

'Are you ready?' he said.

'I'm ready,' she answered.

'Are you willing …?'

'But Mrs Phelps!' pleaded John, 'you'll miss the Maître d's farewell address?!'

'I think I can do without it. Just tip me in, will you, Tony.'

And so like a little heap of sand Tony tipped Mrs Phelps within.

In the main hotel building Tony and John joined the other guests gathered in the foyer awaiting the Maître d'. Out came the man-in-charge, punctual and proud, stood in a kind of mobile pulpit; John had seen one like it before, used by an auctioneer on Anlaby Road in Hull. Although on that occasion there was no large reminder about final gratuities chalked on the front.

'Ladies and gentlemen, boys and girls ...' he began, '... this foyer's a little cold. Trevor, do you think you could push me into the lounge?'

'Why didn't we meet in the lounge to start with?' called out the cowboy, now regained in confidence.

'I think we had enough of your lip last night, didn't we,' admonished the Maître d' as Trevor got the mobile pulpit moving. The cowboy quietened.

In the lounge, people sat and stood about; the full complement of the hotel guests being greater than the number of seats available, by a ratio of 20:9.

'Well,' began the main man, 'first of all I'd like to thank you all for coming. We've had problems ... But I do feel that overall we've operated as a team. There's been a group spirit generated here, and I do hope.'

An abrupt ending but an optimistic one.

Australia, Christmas 2001

Me, Simon and the farm lorry go
down the mountain road from Dorrego,
rattling through rainforest
in the Ute,
en route to Lennox Head
and its Christmas spread of surf.
Simon is at the steering wheel,
our eyes, similarly imperfect.
At the beach under the sun,
I slip my glasses into my swimwear pocket
and dip into the frothing lip of ocean,
but the tide slips inside
and whips away my glasses.
Keen-eyed Janet is good enough
to dive into the sea's heaving haystack,
but they're good and gone.
So, maybe I've made some myopic mermaid better
    looking.

With no spare pair available
and no optician seeing customers on Christmas Day,
Simon is open to a timeshare with his own pair.
Hooray.
My co-wearer's prescription is of different description
but if I tip them at an angle

and don't pull them full on,
the wool over my eyes unstitches;
we're a bit like Shakespeare's witches
who had just one eye between them,
but there's only two of us,
and we're not in Scotland,
we're in Australia,
sharing optical regalia.

It seems the sand is on your chin
which should be on the beach,
it seems some of your spectacles
the darkness couldn't reach

October '71

Today on my eighteenth birthday
my dad gave me a hefty gift in coloured wrapping.
The deftly sealed paper gone
the black tin box revealed:
my father's oil paints.
Inside – the well-thumbed wood of his palette.
I have asked him why he gave up
and here is my answer. He gave up for me to go on.
Here is creativity's baton.
Eyeing the palette, I contemplate
the crusty daubs and splodges
of his concocted shades.
I investigate the metal tubes of pigment.
They are rock solid
and have been so for decades.

November 1973.
A Bradford University student house

Last night was Bonfire Night. We shut ourselves in the kitchen and let off jumping crackers which fizzed and banged around the room in hot pursuit of we the overexcited undergraduates. The others find it particularly amusing that all I have in my food cupboard is a ball of wool. One of the postgrads told me that he used to pull open the door to experience this absurd sight whenever he was feeling depressed; this usually occurred as a result of his fellows stealing from his own neatly packed stock of supplies.

When he discovered that I was the main culprit, my wound wool proved to be less entertaining.

June 1988, Greece

Sunday 3.00 p.m.

Ferry to Siros.

Arrive at port, find bus for Kini.

Man puts our bags in boot of coach – kind man, must be the driver – in fact he is hustler for hotel at the other end (A Marcos). We say *maybe*; we are self-determining individuals. We get on bus, *he* does not. He is forgotten – until we get off the bus and he is standing there with our bags. He has followed the bus, maybe by car, maybe by moped (he does not appear to have been running).

Eurydice speaks

Dog calmed
river crossed –
the gods had made it so clear
look back and she's lost.
So, dog calmed, river crossed
why did he look back?
Was it a chance overshoulder glance,
an absent-minded oversight
that sent me back to Hades,
or was it him checking
to see that I was still there
and then knowing
in that moment of knowing
that I was
but wouldn't be,
or was it an upbraiding glare,
petulance at my following him,
an impulsive reprimand
for which he would reprimand himself
for the rest of his days?
Or was it that he just went nuts?

Or, was it a celebratory sharing,
his foot upon the threshold
he turns ...

'Eurydice, look – we're there ...'
And then only he is there.
The overenthusiastic folly.
The premature judgement.
The complacent Greek.
What was his mistake?
The mistake is yours
if you look only at the possible errors of the man.
With the woman lies the solution.
Yes it happened at the very threshold.
But he turned because ...
because I called him.
And why?
Because I wanted to look at him once more.
But only once.

26.06.00, Medellín

Outside the hotel, I go up to one of the many men with a tray of sweets and tobacco around his neck. I write in the air that I want to buy something to write with. The man shakes his head. So many of these men, so rarely making a sale. I seek elsewhere.

Under the Metro on stilts, around the back of the hotel, other men are laying out their collections of street flotsam, each man a specialist: battered books, old electrical bits; the barely wantable laid out with such consideration and precision. Somewhere back home I have seen art along these lines.

Scotland, 2000

The sinking of the Russian submarine Kirsk had been on my mind all day. Earlier I had been to see Partick Thistle play Stenhuismuir. On the train, I had read in the paper about the Scottish sea captain who was to steer a rescue attempt in his mini-sub. The larger vessel had been on the bottom a long time now, hope was the wrong side of a glimmer. The rescue captain was reported to have admitted it looked grim, but he would do his level best to get to anyone still alive. Level best, he had said. It occurred to me that I did not know the meaning of level best. The captain possibly didn't either. But whatever level best was, he would do it. He knew level best to be an expression of utmost effort.

Even if he did not know the mechanics of the phrase, his level best is what he would do.

At the football game Thistle were given a hiding by the home side.

I stood on the terracing in good company, in good air.

I offered a prayer for the sailors in their other plight.

At one point the ball sailed over our heads and landed behind us in undergrowth.

Boys went fishing. We laughed.

In the bar that night, I asked Simon if he thought those sailors could have laughed. Could someone have said something to slice through the terrible despair? Could they? Simon paused, looked down, and slowly shook his head. And Simon is the optimistic sort.

'Sung!' he said, looking up. 'Maybe they'd have sung.'

That was something. To lift the sunken spirits. If not the sunken sub.

And Nigel imagined the Russian skipper hearing his men break into chorus and ordering them to shut up and stop wasting his oxygen.

From the tube

On the Hammersmith and City Line
I am sat on the floor by the door,
a man gets on
with a neatly folded old blanket beneath his arm,
his hair all of a straggle,
his jacket incomplete,
holes in his deck shoes
with a peep show of his naked feet,
and I think, if I fart now
everyone will think it's him.

Except him.

A Gray day

i

Early afternoon.

Today, I am intending to go and see Luton playing Reading. Life was once one long wedding for me and Luton Town. It's calmed down a lot since those days, but there's still a spark there. Still the possibility of ignition.

After lunch, I'm a little lunched out, wondering whether to attend the game or to laze about the home. No. I should go. I may come away with a glow. I may even grow a little.

Outside the ground, as I queue to get my ticket, minor joy as I hear over the tannoy from within, that Luton will play with Phil Gray. He's the man for me, although not for all it would seem. There is something in him of Cantona; he has style. He does, on occasion, give the ball away, and for this receives big vitriol from the Luton bunch, whom I find less kind than most. 'Go on, Phyllis,' I've heard them say. In a mocking way. Perhaps he is something of an under-dog … but he has played for his country. He is an

Irishman. Luton has a big Irish contingent and I am glad to see them represented.

I'm one of the last in, and there's loads of space. I'll risk selecting a spot superior to my allotted. I catch sight of a pair of gentlemen, ancient, blanket-covered. I feel a small excitement at these old-time Towners and lodge myself behind them. Somehow I share their blanket's warmth.

The game has only just begun when one of these two old gents yells, 'Gray – you muppet!' Imagine the hurt if you were Phil Gray's dad and you heard that. Imagine if he was *your* dad. Your own dad – no more than a muppet! Horrible. But I'm not moving now.

Luton score a scrappy goal. I feel no happiness and despair that I'm losing my connection with the team altogether.

'We' go in 1–0 up at half-time and I go down to get my half-time cuppa, despondent.

ii

In the second half. The stakes are raised. Reading equalise. A rising of temperatures. I'm interested now.

Very near my vantage, I see Phil Gray up close, going for a 50–50 ball and knocking down his younger marker, a fair challenge but robust. He helps the felled one to his feet and rubs his hair in a sporting way. This man is no underdog. This dog is hot. The other player's name is Gray too, as an even younger lad behind me enthusiastically indicates, programme open, on the lap of perhaps his grandad. The Town pressurise, Gray fashions a sudden turn and a shot out of nothing – out of true class. There is no appreciation from the muppeteer – these are hard times, this is a hard town, a hard game and hard, hard seating. Come on, Town – Come on, Phil Gray – Come on, my son.

In a sustained attacking spell the ball comes out to my man: control, poise, shoot, power, precision. It's there! The voice comes to my throat without the asking. I'm right up. I'm giving it some. And so is the jeering muppet-man – muppeting no longer. We're all in it together. I am lost and found in the ground, in the crowing crowd. The hunger is fed. The whole is fixed. And the goal is disallowed.

It's

It's the wheel that squeaks
that gets the oil.
It's boil up the beetroot
not the soil.
It's death you can't cheat
but you can eat it.
It's hard to hear the worm
above the turmoil.
It's the unspoken desire that is the stronger,
it's the longing that I long to have again,
it's the falling autumn leaf that never knows what it
    is losing,
it's the heating of your winter feet
that lives you with a chilblain.
It's the wheel that squeaks
that gets the oil,
it's the gobbing and the yobbing,
it's the robbing of the innocence
it's dibbing and it's dobbing
down the pan,
it's the time to tell a copper
that the world has come a cropper
'Look it's time to put a stopper
in it man.'
It's the wheel that squeaks

that gets the oil,
it's the creaking keel which I prefer,
the wood seems like it's living,
it's the man who's on his mobile
sat adjacent in the carriage
who is making me feel
ever so estranged,
it's my inky pair of trousers
from a biro that was leaking,
it's the stain upon my t-shirt,
from a wheel I'm often dealing with –
a wheel I think, it's time, perhaps, I changed.

1999. London. Mud. Winter.

In the pub for Sunday-night chatter with chums.

The Scot in our midst tells a jest in which a biblical chapter and verse reference is required to give his story a flourish of detail. He plucks one at random. The Australian with us has a Bible handy. I ask if she would read out the selected text. The Scotsman says it was randomly selected. I say nothing is done at random – I mean, nothing occurs by chance and without significance. The Aussie reads; the passage tells of the Lord bestowing sight after placing mud upon the lids of the deprived. In my mind's eye I am seeing this mud being taken from a potato, an aspect of the healing unrevealed in the text.

Moorfields Eye Hospital

I am sat in the waiting room, glancing at the eyes of the other patients, trying to catch sight of their reasons for being there, without them discovering this small espionage. Like the doctors, I am looking for corneal inflammation, dandruff of the eyelashes, that kind of thing.

I discover that I am in possession of a Meiobian Cyst.

'It's got three heads,' says the doctor, telling me to collect ointment from the hospital's own pharmacy. I follow the direction on the big sign saying PHARMACY – DROPS AND OINTMENTS. In the queue the woman in front of me turns and says, 'It's very warm in here, isn't it?'

'Yes,' I reply, and, feeling I should add something further, 'What are you getting, drops or ointment?'

'Ointment,' says the woman. 'And you?'

'Ointment,' I answer, enjoying for a moment this fraction of shared destiny.

Toffee lover

There once was a woman of Bracknell
who loved eating pieces of cracknel.
'It's bad for your teeth,'
said her dentician, Keith,
although her sweet tooth wasn't the only part of her
which this unusually shy man found sweet – sub-
sequently he was quietly glad of their regular albeit
infrequent appointments.

Ipswich

Waiting at my table
in Ipswich,
the lips which

I wanted

to touch mine.

The hips which
I wanted
to swing with.

I wanted to sing with you,
but instead of song
all I did was say
politely
that the chips which
you laid before me
were slightly undercooked.

In the headlights of your beauty
heading for the dip-switch.
The coin flips which way?
The wrong way?
No.

For I go back to Ipswich,
having left the train at Chelmsford.

Keeping your distance

Like the enchanting seaside pebble
which becomes ordinary in the pocket,

Like the fly-sheet of a tent, touched,
and the seal is broken,

Like the hungry, very angry dog
enjoying its bone,
or its potato.

Like all of these,
you
were best
left
alone.

Blancmange

He's a man who prefers to have something blancmange
whenever he has a dessert,
he gets what he can in his tummy,
he tries to get none on his shirt.
If there's ever blancmange as an option,
blancmange is the option he'll take,
there have been occasions when money's changed hands
to encourage the kitchen to make
something blancmange.
I asked him one day
in a casual way
what made blancmange so top-notch:
the gobbling … or was it the wobbling, I wondered,
which stirred something down in the crotch?
He answered, 'It may seem absurd,
but the thing that I love
is the word: blancmange,
it's French
and it's funny as well,
to me it's enchanting
as you can see, I am under its wonderful spell.
It's the pet name I gave to the love of my life
who has splintered my heart
like a fist might
a freshly blown egg shell.'

In attempting to draw from memory the scene depicted by my father,
I have represented Le Bar de la Treille one storey short of reality.

The sound of paint drying

On my wall there is a small picture of a street scene in France, painted long before I was born, by an amateur watercolourist. The focus is a five-storey vine-clad building, with a bar at the bottom; the name is visible on the sign – Le Bar de la Treille – the bar with the trellis. There are a couple of barrels and a quintet of people. Facing the bar is a brown-hatted man. There is blue sky, there are green railings. In the bottom right-hand corner is the artist's signature – R. Hegley, Vieux Nice 1931.

The picture I usually paint of my father
is the one of him smacking me as a lad:
hard and uncompromising.
It is not a lie but neither is it the only angle
from which one can capture his portrait.

Other brush strokes reveal a man born in France,
to a French mother – a man, who in his twenties
made gentle, playful, colourful portraits of his
        native land.

In 1905
my dad was alive

but he wasn't alive before this,
his mum used to dance with the Folies-Bergère
and she was a native of Paris.

My grandad gave my father
his Anglo-Irish name,
it seems he gave him little else
which is a shame,
but I don't apportion blame;
Grandma called her son René Robert,
although Bob's what he later became.

My father painted canvases,
his mum played mandolin:
the artiness was in the blood
and sometimes, on the skin.

*

We find my father sat in Nice
when he was twenty-six,
he's poking at some canvas
with his range of hairy sticks.
First he takes his pencil
and he outlines what he sees;
proportion and perspective by degrees,
then turning to his brushes,
to the narrow and the stout,

he puts them in the pigment
as he wiggles them about.
And it's highly naturalistic,
it is not impressionistic
it is not expressionistic
neither futurist nor fauve
it isn't pointillistic,
it is highly naturalistic,
in places it is orange
and in others it is mauve.

4 May 2001

On the plane to Nice from Luton. My intention is to
paint the scene my father painted, or whatever scene is
in its place. If the whole street has been turned into an
office, then I will paint the wall. I have a sore throat. I
have a supply of Strepsils. Normally, I buy the red ones
– Strepsils Original – but for my French visit I have
gone for yellow Strepsils. I believe life favours the one
who takes risks. I have no painting equipment: I will
purchase it in France.

   Why do I embark upon this journey?

   To take up my father's tools.

   To know the fixing of line and the mixing of colour
as he knew it.

To visit the town I know he loved.

I cherish the fragment of Frenchness which I have through my father's birthplace (Paris), his name (René) and his French mother (Maman). In doing this painting I hope to claim something of this inheritance – and to find out by treading in my father's footsteps something about my own feet.

5 May

Nice.

My paints I purchase from a shop patronised by Matisse himself – and possibly by my own old master. I joke with the vendor about the expense of his equipment, his pencils in particular, adding that at least the water will be free. He is only very mildly amused.

Seeking out the site of my father's creation, I find the same street and the same bar are still in place – the bar has a new name, but there is the very vine which clawed its way up his watercolour, seventy years previous. And there is the same iron railing whose intricacies he wrought. And still it is painted green. The whole of this ancient part of town is much as he left it; the most noticeable modern addition is the graffiti – cosmetic – although you wouldn't want it on your face.

6 May

I set up with my equipment outside what was once Le Bar de la Treille. It is a sunny morning. My throat is more sore; still, I have had my coffee and curved croissant. It is ten o'clock. I set my pad upon my knee, I open my clean array of oblong colours. When asking for a pencil in the shop, the patron recommended 5H – *very hard*; I didn't want to contradict generations of experience and followed his direction. But I also bought a 5B pencil – a Mister Softy. I want my formative lines to be clear. I look at the leafy building before me, I survey its angles. I consider its shadows. I get the sense of it – as my old dad would have done. I begin.

*

My father's painting is very traditional and also very competent. What is of particular note is the working of the detail, as though it's been done on a massive scale and then reduced accordingly. As though the tiny is home. As I make my piece I realise my shortcomings as a brushmaster. I get despondent early on, but stay with it. And then, working on the sky, as I pop a new yellow Strepsil into my mouth to ease my aching, I know what I must do. Out comes the Strepsil and on to my newly painted blueness it goes. Mixed-media – watercolour and throat sweet. And the sun is in the sky and the son understands his place in things. Not the fine brushworker, the steady builder – that was my dad. I go on with renewed incentive. Don't just know your limitations. Love them.

My father was a painter. I am an idiot.

*

1.00 p.m. Outdoors at a nearby restaurant, awaiting some lunch, the sun smiles upon my near-completed painting which I'm looking at now upon my lap. In the interval before my meal's arrival I decide to put a figure on the street. I decide to depict the hatted man from my father's painting. The same man but, unlike Dad, I depict him with his back to the café, facing front. After much fiddling, the man is finished. I realise that he is me. He doesn't look much like me, but nor does my painting of the street look much like the street. The man is me. I draw him a dog.

And that's why I came here. For an art of necessity. I painted this picture to find myself. I found myself. And my dog.

After lunch, I return to the scene, to add the last details to my piece. Someone from a café opposite the one I'm painting comes and has a look. He seems affirmative. He indicates that he has other paintings of the voluptuous vine inside. I discover that they are mostly more modern, but there is one that is older. 1930. It is a colour copy. The signature in the bottom right-hand corner is R. Dufy – French Impressionist, Raoul Dufy.

Something which has come to light, as my own work has progressed, is the physical point of view of my father's painting. It would seem to be not from the street, but from the window of the building opposite. I have little detail of his life at this time. I knew he was here with my grandmother. Is this where they lived? A sequence of events suggests itself: One morning, a year before he paints the scene, my father looks out of the window and sees below him a man at work with watercolours. This other man seems happy, engrossed, fulfilled. Like I have been. But it is not me. It is not necessary for my father to find me through some ludicrous somersault of time. It is Dufy, whom my father watches. Perhaps my father has never yet put his thumb through the palette; but now he is hooked. I'll have some of that, he thinks, in French – and the following year he is at it himself, after an argument with the man in the art shop about the extortionate price of his pencils.

*

Last night, I picked my father's painting off the wall. I had still believed there to be only four figures outside that bar. I now knew there to be five. Now, the woman was stooping over her wares, with a sale a possibility. Previously she had merely been stooping, maybe looking at some flowers, maybe rearranging them, but now she would seem to be entering into a process of exchange. This insubstantial man would seem to be spending money. We make our guesses and our assumptions. He is glad of good value. He is probably buying flowers, possibly fruit, maybe pencils. Cheap pencils.

*

I have been asked, what is inside the two barrels
resting on the pavement.

Let me tell you.
In the barrels
there are bees.
Stripy bees.

The woman in the stripy apron
is shortly to turn
and free
the barrelled bee-life.

She'll make a bee-line
for the bee-life
in what used to be the tree-life,
with her knife.
And the man
at the front of it all
is still trying to comprehend
her beauty,
a man who has never travelled up the Eiffel Tower.
'It is every Frenchman's duty,' he will say,
asking her to accompany him
up to that famous above
where he'll fall in love with her,
and call her sweet, so sweet – his blancmange.

Suddenly a hurled potato breaches
a window in Le Bar de la Treille.
The owner rapidly appears in search of a culprit.
The leaning man indicates the ripped face
peering from the pasted poster.
'It was him!' he accuses, in the lingo of France,
whilst beginning to dance.
'It's nothing to dance about! Nothing!'
opposes the patron.
'Dancing needs not wait upon occasion,
it is the natural state of the human animal,'
explains the dancing man.
The bar-proprietor returns to his domain,
picks up the offending potato,

holds it to his ear
and listens
to the sound of the ground
from whence it came.

Tu vas me manquer,
ma petite

The above is written in the hand of my French teacher, Juliette, who
thus translated 'I'm going to miss you, my little one'. It is notable that
the French put the beloved first: the self is superseded by the other,
by the passion, by the potato.

Jesus is not just for Christmas

Down in the Bible
some of it's tribal,
a tooth for a tooth
and eyeball for an eyeball,
some of it's truth, some of it's Gospel:
a man with a mission, a mission impospel,
a man with a tan, a man who liked a parable,
cast your seed on to land that is arable,
a stony field and the yield will be tarrable.
Born in a manger, born into danger,
don't take gifts from any old stranger
especially if it's gold.
Especially if they say you've been specially selected
and they've found your address by following a star
with a couple of mates who've got gifts as well –
      unusual gifts:
just tell 'em – 'Thanks, but no ta.'

Did he have a sweet tooth, did he have a sweetheart,
when he was a youth, did he do some street art?
Did he have a dog, was it a disaster,
breaking all its legs and going round in plaster?
Swallowed by the water, following its master,
Sinking like a stone, only sinking somewhat faster?

He had his staff, to help him with his walkin',
he had his staff, to do some of the talkin'.
He had his path, it never had a fork in,
he made a lot of sandwiches and none of them had
    pork in.
If you had a party he knew how to cater,
he could feed a party with the one potater:
'Don't go thanking me, mate, credit The Creator.'
'The wine's all gone, son', 'Don't you worry, mater,
let me have that water for a moment, would you,
    waiter?'

Down in the temple, kicking up a rumpus,
money-lenders wondering, 'Is he going to thump us?
He don't like us, is he gonna lump us,
spilling our blood all over our new jumpers?'

Treated like a criminal, flattened in a hymninal,
what the men don't do, maybe the women'll
do.

A proper dad, he never really had one.
It's not on file if the child was a glad one,
No trial – for whatever it was the lad done,
if that's a Good Friday, I wouldn't want a bad one.

Cyprus, October '94

In the hotel.

Jackie is pregnant.

'That's no normal fly,' she complains, anxiously. 'He's doing a funny somersault, please kill him; he's a biter.' Earlier, in the *Rough Guide* I was reading about how a local Roman ruin was used as a quarry by fifteenth-century builders. One man's quarry stone is another man's slab of venerable antiquity. Similarly, one man's meat is one small parasite's fast-food diner.

Today is my birthday. This morning Jackie presented me with a pile of gifts purchased from the market. The first one I opened was a pair of sandals. I exclaimed that this is the sort of pressie a Roman might have received. As the unveiling proceeds, I pronounce each item to have been a possibility in Roman times:

Little picture frame with dogs depicted on the edges.

Cashew nuts.

Keyrings (two for some reason, one with my phone number on, which I must admit would be an unlikely addition in Roman times, unless it was an Emperor's keyring of course).

Ceramic eggcup with a candle inside.

Sandals (tiny ones on the other keyring).

Nivea Cream, Made in Cyprus, in a tin with a
     painted boat on it.
Cloth rose with affectionate note attached.
Beer mat.
Mints.

Coming down from Stavros Mountain, Jackie is going
through possible names for the newborn. 'What about
Thomas? I like Francesca ...'

When we get back to Polis, where we are staying,
I want to go to the men's café, where they play backgammon.

'... Do you think *Josephine* is nice?'

The elderly are more socially integrated here and
some are whizzo at backgammon.

'... Josephine's a French name, isn't it?'

When we were in the restaurant the other night a large
extended family was celebrating an eighteen-year-
old's birthday; the birthday girl brought us cake and I
yearned for the kind of social belonging they have
here.

We are sat outside the café now. It's six o'clock, but
dark already. I write this in sparse light. Jackie says we
need more soap. In the café someone slaps a backgammon piece down with conviction. On the way to
the café, on the floor, I found an old wooden lollystick,

broken in two, and made into a cross bound at the centre by elastic bands. Probably Roman. Someone next to me has turned on their motorcycle headlights; it gives me more light to write in. Jackie is reading *Middlemarch* under a beautiful tree. A man has come out of the café; I want to ask him what kind of tree it is but feel he might think I'm being stupid or too forward. I will ask the café owner. With him I have entered into an economic relationship and I feel entitled to broach the issue. Jackie says she is getting bitten; she is going to have a slow poodle home and is going to buy some soap on the way. Before she leaves, a last wild choice at child naming. 'What about Stavros?'

The new father's mistake

In the hospital
the new mother has agreed
to assist in testing the worth
of a new natal drug.
Soon after the birth
the marvellous midwife gives me the relevant
    questionnaire to hold
and proceeds to organise her patient's relative comfort.
I mistakenly think she has told me to complete
the sheet.
Inwardly I express surprise
that my responses are of interest, but feel it best
not to question the interests of modern science.
I proceed to give my answers in
dutiful compliance.
Marking is from nought to five
depending on how intensely
the phenomenon described
is thought to have been experienced.
The following represents how it was for me.
Headaches – nought
Abdominal pain – nought
Nausea – nought
Shivering – nought
Vomiting – nought
Tiredness – five.

Early dealings with our daughter

That morning
she is a month old,
I hold on to her littleness
and ask her, 'Where are your teeth?
Where are they, where are your teeth?'
It may seem a daft question
but so is any question to someone her age.
Anyway, that afternoon
we are visited by friends
and when they have gone, I am told,
'Imelda says her teeth are coming through.'
'Really,' I reply,
'I was asking her about her teeth only this morning.'

Dancing in Luton

My family was not big on dancing in my boyhood Luton. I never danced to my daddy, nor he to me. As a father myself I have tried to do better in this department. When I was first practising my potato dance, my daughter would bring her own spuds in from the kitchen and flourish them to the recording of Nigel's Portuguese guitar tones. Not always in time. But always intense. For some while after, she associated all dance with potatoes, and on the occasion of an impromptu domestic disco session, she hurried off to make her selections from the organic vegetable basket.

Song for two dads

She wants to fly,
up in the sky.
She wants to fly.
But not too high.

Not like the lad with the dad in mythology
who told him just stay away from the sun,
or the wax in the feathers will melt in the weather
and down you will plummet and you'll be undone.

Talking of flying and tales of mythology,
what of the moth that did flutter and flit
into and out of the tales of mythology?
… What of it?

I am that moth
that moth of myth,
that moth I am
that milligram.
I am the moth, the moth of ages,
I've read the books
and eaten the pages.

Did you have a piece of the fleece that was golden?
I did, but I found it devoid of all taste,

much more appealing was Hercules' wardrobe,
his pants in particular, I laid to waste.

And what of your family,
how is your progeny?
Thank you for asking, the family's fine.
My child she likes flapping her arms about wildly
as if she would fly away.
So too does mine.

London N1, '99

Walking across Newington Green
yards from where I was born,
I am teaching my daughter,
aged four and a quarter,
the tune of Dizzy Gillespie's 'A Night in Tunisia'.
'You don't know what jazz is, do you?' I say.
And she says, 'What is it?'
And I say it is a style of music
and a way of being.
And she says, 'A style of music
and a way of being?
Mm ... interesting.'

More Roman numerals

i

Isabella is six.
With her coloured sticks she is doing a drawing
of she and her best friend.

When it is done, I observe that
what is of particular note is the working of the detail,
as though it's been done on a massive scale
and then reduced accordingly.
As though the tiny is home.

ii

She resents me
going away to perform my poems.
I've tried to make amends for my absence
with games played on the phone:
hangman, noughts and crosses,
and making stupid noises for the other person to copy.

When I was gone to Australia,
she came to stay for a bit.

She had no wish to hear me say poetry,
but enjoyed taking the lift up to our accommodation,
always selecting buttons
other than the one for our floor.
When she went home to England
how I missed her small pushiness,
how dull, as I pressed the predictable number,
and no more.

The party spirito

A lovely hilltop village party
above the seaside of Sestri le Vanti:
beer, chianti,
aubergine, spaghetti
and pesto on bread like chapatti.
The band play the cha-cha
and what sounds to me like Italian village party music.
They play it well.
The partygoers swell
To maybe six hundred.
The time is after ten,
Now we leave, to spread the small children
in their bedtime.
Hermione, who is two,
has a question:
'What about the candles?'
It is understandable.
It is a party, after all.
Approaching the cars
she says she wants to blow them out.
She is referring to the stars.

My son

Close to the end of the Fringe Festival in Edinburgh,
it was reported in the *Scotsman*
that I had left before the end of a performance
accompanied by my small son.
Up until this point,
I had no son.
I greeted his coming
with anointing breath.
It's a boy!
It's joy!
And it's a Scot:

You've been a naughty boy
disappearing like that,
where have you been?
Where are you?
Where's your mum?
Who's your mum? ...

Excuse me, madam,
this isn't your son, is it?
I'm trying to find his mum.

I can't see him either, madam.

He's there, though,
it said so in the Scotsman.
Are you his mum?

Cardiff

In Cardiff,
Chris and Matt
are sat
in a boat
on the river.
'One does find it hardiff
one is treated with such disregard,'
complains Chris.
'STUFF THAT.'
moans Matt.
The toff
and the tough
have a tiff
on the Taff.